My Sister, My Friend

Sherry Ramrattan Smith

 FriesenPress

Suite 300 - 990 Fort St
Victoria, BC, Canada, V8V 3K2
www.friesenpress.com

ISBN
978-1-4602-7975-5 (Paperback)
978-1-4602-7976-2 (eBook)

1. Juvenile Nonfiction, Family

Distributed to the trade by The Ingram Book Company

To Madyn and Mila

May your best dreams find their way to you.

Sherry ☺

My sister is the most beautiful baby I have ever seen.

She loves to take naps
and so do I.

We spend a lot of time
napping together.

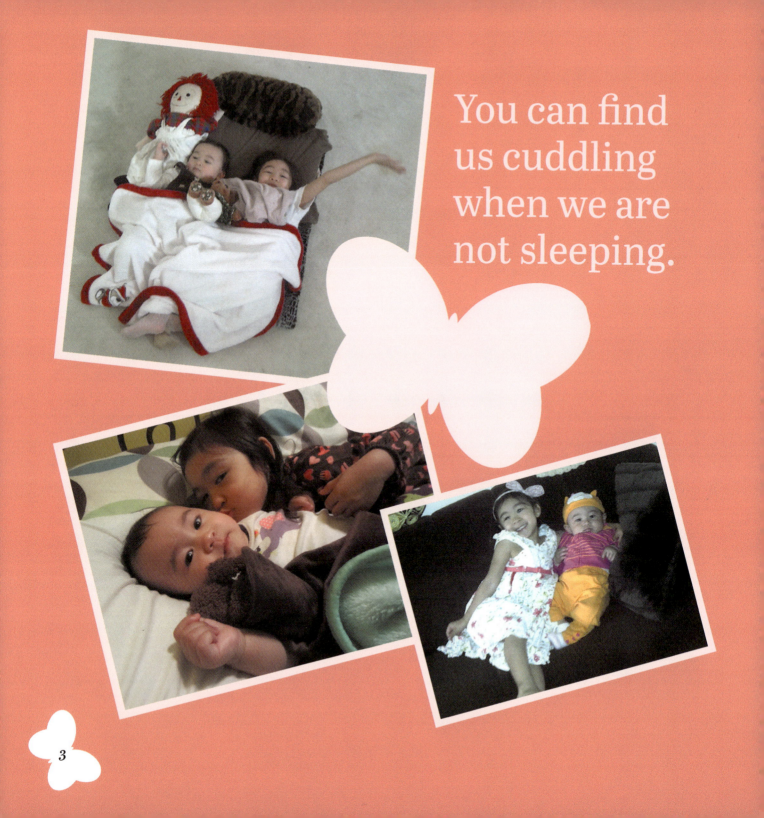

You can find us cuddling when we are not sleeping.

We like to
dress up
for tea.

My sister still lets me hug her
even when I act silly.

We like to share all types of food especially pizza and ice cream.

6

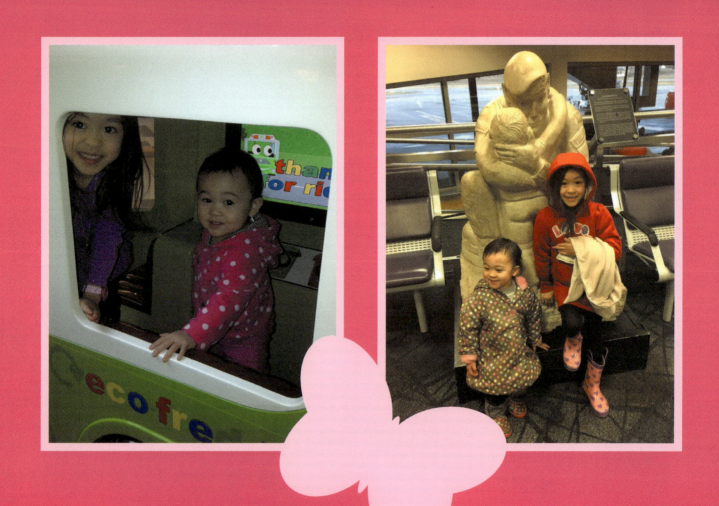

We play in a minivan at the mall.
Sometimes we travel
together on a family trip.

We think that
slides are fun!

We go for walks,

climb rocks,

and pick out
cool stones to collect.

When we get tired
we sit and rest.

9

We have fun with
Sparky at Grandpa and
Grandma's home.

We love to dance.
My sister gives
me a flower as a
special gift after
my dance recital.

We enjoy all types of celebrations. At Halloween we pick out pumpkins to carve. We dress up as a zebra and a cow. Another time, we dress up as Ariel and a pig. We have fun saying *trick or treat.*

At Christmas we
pose with Santa Claus
for a photograph.

In winter
we have
fun in the
snow.

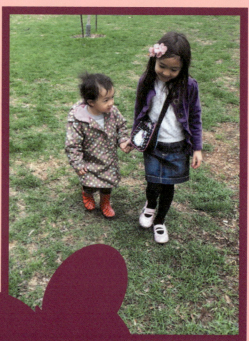

The best part of each day is when we just hang out together.

17

We are sisters and *we love each other*.

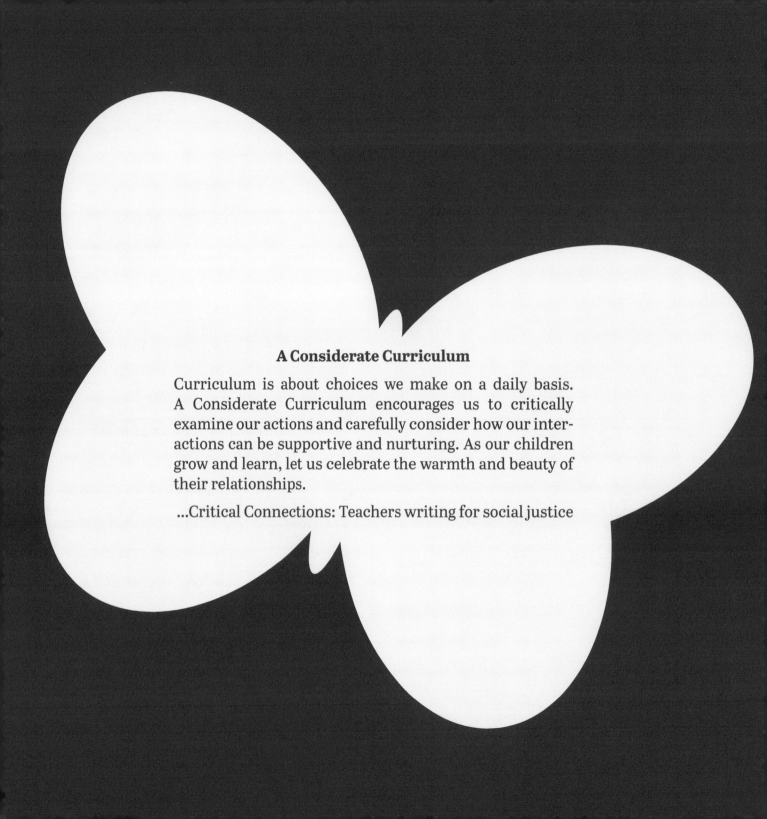

A Considerate Curriculum

Curriculum is about choices we make on a daily basis. A Considerate Curriculum encourages us to critically examine our actions and carefully consider how our interactions can be supportive and nurturing. As our children grow and learn, let us celebrate the warmth and beauty of their relationships.

...Critical Connections: Teachers writing for social justice

CPSIA information can be obtained
at www.ICGtesting.com
Printed in the USA
LVIC04n1326030216
473417LV00007B/40

9 781460 279755